THE HOUSE ON THE KLONG

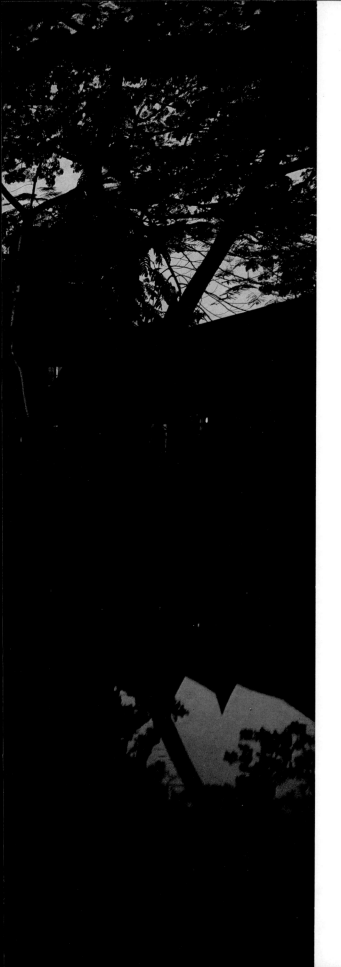

THE HOUSE
ON
THE KLONG

*The Bangkok Home and
Asian Art Collection
of James Thompson*

photographs
BRIAN BRAKE

text
WILLIAM WARREN

Privately Printed: Tokyo, 1968

This book was originally commissioned by James Thompson, proceeds from its sale to be used for charity. Following his disappearance, the commission has been renewed by his family. Other than the biographical note and its accompanying portraits, which have now been added, the book is very much as James Thompson planned it.

———◄•●•►———

This copy is specially bound in Thai silk. The photograph mounted on the binding reproduces a painting by Somnuk Permthongkum, one of the few young Thai artists who still paint in the traditional style; it shows various stages of silk weaving in a house on a klong.

First edition, January, 1968
Seventh printing, March, 1973

Copyright in Japan, 1968, by James Thompson
Produced by John Weatherhill, Inc., Tokyo, Japan
Printed in Japan

Library of Congress Catalog Card No.68-20640

THE HOUSE ON THE KLONG

A CHARACTERISTIC of Asian cities which has traditionally frustrated Western visitors is their tendency to hide their treasures from public view: to contradict, at first glance, their legends of splendor. Generations of travelers have felt, on their introduction to Rangoon or Singapore or Bangkok, as Somerset Maugham did when he made a trip through the Orient in the 1920's: "They are all alike, with their straight streets, their arcades, their tramways, their dust, their blinding sun . . . their dense traffic, their ceaseless din. . . . They are hard and glittering and as unreal as a backcloth in a musical comedy. They give you nothing. But when you leave them it is with a feeling that you have missed something and you cannot help thinking that they have some secret that they have kept from you."

The tendency remains today, though the exteriors of the cities have changed. What bewilders and depresses the present-day visitor is not so much that all Asian cities look alike but that all cities, Asian or otherwise, are similar. Architecture, along with so many other things, has become international, and it is increasingly difficult to tell whether one is in Asia or the West. The real treasures, meanwhile, have become even less visible to the traveler, the secrets a little more difficult to pry out of their glittering guardians.

But they are still there, amid all the familiar things, and they have not lost their power to surprise and enchant when discovered. In Bangkok, after sadly noting the city's "dust and heat and noise and whiteness and more dust," Maugham came upon its traditional temple architecture, and before those "incredible buildings" the monotony of the modern city faded away: "They are unlike anything in the world, so that you are taken aback, and you cannot fit them into the scheme of the things you know. It makes you laugh with delight to think that anything so fantastic could exist on this sombre earth. . . . I do not know that these Siamese wats have beauty, which they say is reserved and aloof and very refined; all I know is that they are strange and gay and odd, their lines are infinitely distinguished, like the lines of a proposition in a schoolboy's Euclid, their colors are flaunting and crude, like the colors of vegetables in the greengrocer's stall at an open-air market, and, like a place where seven ways meet, they open roads down which the imagination can make many a careless and unexpected journey."

In Maugham's time, had he looked a little further, down the klongs, or canals, that then threaded through the city, he would have found hundreds of residential buildings in a similar style, the domestic equivalents of the temples, and he would undoubtedly have been just as delighted with them. Today, finding them is not such a simple matter. The temples themselves are still there, as strange and bright as ever behind their thick, protective walls, but it takes a determined visitor to ferret out the old houses in their hiding places, often in the shadow of some massive, commonplace modern structure and just as often suffering from neglect. For this reason, a visitor who comes across James H. W. Thompson's residence, just a block away from the National Stadium, is in a sense doubly rewarded: he has the pleasure of finding one of those unexpected treasures in an unlikely place, and he also has a chance to see an example of an architectural form that, if it is not actually dying, is at least certainly threatened by what is usually called progress.

Even a casual comparison shows that Thai religious and domestic architecture have much in common and, indeed, the elaborate temples, or wats, very probably took their original inspiration from the simpler village houses that surrounded them. Both have the same quality of lightness, of seeming to strain to touch the sky; both have the same rather surprising combination of fancy and practicality. The religious buildings have absorbed more influences from other cultures, however, and have become far more complex, both in design and in function. The Indians during the earliest period, the Khmers during the five centuries they ruled part of the country, the Burmese who built in the north, and the Chinese who came in later years, all left their marks on the style; though the ultimate synthesis, which came to its full flowering in the Ayudhya period (fourteenth to late eighteenth century) was quite distinctly Thai in feeling and appearance.

The domestic architecture of the country, though borrowing certain decorative features from other cultures, remained essentially simple, based primarily on easily available building materials, on the climate, and on the needs of the people, mostly farmers, who lived in it. The most available material for building was wood, which, in the case of the better houses, meant the hard, long-lasting teak of the northern forests. The tropical climate dictated the airy, open quality of Thai houses and the broad over-hangs of the roof, which protect the interior from both the sun and the rains; it is also responsible for the fact that the houses are raised off the ground, safe from rainy-season floods as well as from wild animals. In a provincial house, the open area beneath is used for keeping animals, for storing crops, or as a living room in the hot season.

There are relatively few purely decorative touches in Thai houses, and even those are strikingly simple; unlike the temples, the domestic buildings never adopted the dazzling colors of the Chinese, who introduced to the religious architecture such features as glazed tiles and lavish use of gold leaf. The curved roof-ends of the houses, which add so much to their graceful appearance, are probably adaptations of the nagas, or serpents, that adorn Khmer temples, though they have been so stylized as to bear little resem-blance to the originals. The only other really non-useful decorations are the panels of carved wood, often Chinese in style, which are found under the windows and above the doors in some houses, generally in the more expen-sive ones. The raised thresholds, while they may have a symbolic purpose (to keep evil spirits from entering the rooms), also have a structural function in keeping the wall firmly in place.

The entire house is built in light, pre-fabricated sections, which are hung on the superstructure without nails; thus it can be taken down and moved with comparative ease, which, in the old days, was very often done. The supporting columns and, consequently, the walls as well are inclined toward the center. The practical purpose of this is uncertain, but aesthetically it adds greatly to the illusion of height and elegance which is perhaps the most memorable feature of traditional Thai architecture.

The original Thompson house and outbuildings were assembled from six separate old houses and came to their present location from a variety of sources. The oldest part of the main house, the large drawing room, came from the silk-weaving village of Bang Krua across the klong, which was a village long before Bangkok expanded and swallowed it. The house was built around 1800 and served several generations of a weaving family; in

1957, it was owned by five heirs, each of whom wanted his own house and all of whom agreed to sell the old structure so as to build separate new ones. The next oldest part, the kitchen wing, dates from around the middle of the nineteenth century and was originally part of a palace which was moved about fifty years ago to Bang Krua.

What is now the entrance stairhall, the dining room, the master bedroom, and the bathroom walls of the main house consists of houses found in a village called Pak Hai, northwest of the old capital city of Ayudhya; they are approximately sixty years old and got to Bangkok by river stacked on barges. Another building from Pak Hai was used to construct the connecting links between the various sections, the ground-floor panels of the entrance hall, and the gardener's house in the back of the compound. The cook's house to the left of the gate leading into the compound came from Banglampoo, a district of Bangkok, and is about fifty years old. The only non-Thai part of the main house is the carved partition wall between the drawing room and the master bedroom wing; it was formerly the entrance to a Chinese pawnshop in Bangkok.

The terrace off the drawing room and the paths of the upper garden are paved with seventeenth-century brick from Ayudhya; the green tiles in the parapet of the terrace are Chinese and also from Ayudhya, to which they came as ballast in the rice boats returning from trade in China, probably in the eighteenth century. The carved pediments in the klongside landing came from the town of Prachinburi.

Several years ago, the main house was expanded by the addition of a second guest room, which also came from Pak Hai, and another small house was added to the far left-hand corner of the property to house a collection of old paintings of daily Thai life.

The site of the house, while it is today largely indistinguishable from the rest of metropolitan Bangkok, was once part of a spacious compound occupied by the Kasemsong family's summer palace; in those days the area was in the country and people went there to get away from the noise and heat of the city. The klong that runs past it was dug in the early part of the nineteenth century and is known as Maha Nag, or Big Naga, the name being inspired by the serpentine twists it takes before coming to Klong Krung Kasem, which formed the original boundary of Bangkok.

The main house departs from traditional Thai architecture in several ways, some of them in the interests of greater comfort and some for aesthetic purposes. In a pure Thai house, the various rooms would be separate units connected by open walkways, and the staircase would be outside; the connecting corridors and the enclosed entrance hall of the Thompson residence were added for the sake of convenience. Also, a traditional house would probably be unpainted, outside and inside. This custom has been followed with the interior walls, which have been left their natural teak color, but the outside is painted with a dull-red creosote which has been a popular preservative in Thailand since its introduction from England in the last century. The walls of the drawing room have been reversed, so that the carving under the window frames faces the inside.

The bathrooms, in which Thai marble is used, are of course concessions to modern life. The old Italian marble in the entrance hall and the crystal chandelier in the drawing room would not be found in most Thai houses, but they are not quite as anachronistic as they might first appear: both were found in Bangkok palaces where they, like so many other Western decorative effects, found their way in the nineteenth century.

Work on the superstructure of the main house was begun on September 15, 1958, and with the blessing of the abbot of Wat Kreuwan, it was officially completed on April 3, 1959.

The construction of any house in Thailand, and of most public buildings as well, entails a number of religious ceremonies which, while they are several steps removed from pure Buddhist belief, are nonetheless considered important to the future comfort and security of the occupants. All these ceremonies were observed in building the Thompson house.

The first is held when the house is begun. In Thompson's case, this was performed by a Brahmin priest and nine Buddhist priests from Ayudhya, who chanted prayers while the initial wooden column was raised and later placed bowls of food around the property to persuade the earth spirits to keep the house secure.

The second involves finding a suitable location for the spirit house, a miniature replica of a house or temple in which the spirits of the compound are supposed to dwell and without which most Thai compounds would feel incomplete. Deciding on a site is a matter that must properly be determined by a qualified Brahmin priest, not by the owner of the property, and is important because a wrongly placed spirit house may result in a variety of misfortunes for the residents. In the Thompson compound, it took one morning to find a place that met all the requirements, one of which is that the shadow of the main house is not supposed to fall across it; the priest also prepared a genealogical chart on the compound spirits, carrying their history back 2,000 years. The little house, set on a post, is located in the far right-hand corner of the compound, overlooking the klong and shaded by a Flame of the Forest tree; offerings of fresh flowers and food are made daily to keep the spirits content, and small clay figures of humans and animals are provided to serve their symbolic needs.

The final ceremony, by far the most important, is the one marking the completion of the house. There are lucky and unlucky days and months for moving into a house (just as there are for getting married, going on a trip, and opening a new business) and the selection of a propitious date is a complex job in which astrological charts are consulted; in many cases it may prove to be before or some time after the actual completion of the building. On the chosen day, an odd number of priests, usually seven or nine—it was nine with the Thompson house—perform the chanting, and a senior priest supervises a number of purification rites. A symbolic cord, which must not be broken, is stretched around the perimeter of the property and connected to each of the buildings on it; spots of sacred sandalwood powder and gold leaf are applied to all the principal doors and to the forehead of the owner; lustral water is sprinkled about the premises; and the ceremony is climaxed by a luncheon for the priests and invited guests. Following this, the house is deemed ready for habitation.

While the Thompson house was built primarily as a home for its owner, an American who has lived in Thailand since 1945, it also serves as a suitable setting for his extensive collection of Asian art, which has been one of his main interests since he took up residence in this part of the world. The variety of this collection is considerable, ranging as it does from Cambodian deities to Chinese porcelains, but for the purposes of discussion it might be divided into statuary and paintings, porcelains, furniture, and what, for lack of a more precise word, is perhaps best gathered under "Miscellaneous."

The sculpture in the house is all from Southeast Asia, principally from Thailand and Cambodia; there are a few Burmese pieces, such as the tall wooden figures and the seated gold-lacquer Buddha in the drawing room. The more important objects are pictured and described elsewhere in this book, though it might be useful here to mention some that catch the eye of even a casual visitor to the house: the sixth-century torso in the garden off the entrance hall, believed to be one of the earliest images of the Buddha found in Southeast Asia; the large U-Thong-style head in the drawing room, an exceptionally handsome example of that period; the beautiful green-sandstone image of the Buddha, Dvaravati period, in the study; and the fine stone figures of Siva and his consort Uma in the niches outside the dining room. In terms of time, the collection covers some fourteen centuries and contains fine examples of most of the important styles in Southeast Asian art.

The traditional Thai paintings in the main house represent an art that is largely unknown in the West and that is, except for a few contemporary painters, almost dead in Thailand itself. The paintings in the Thompson collection are on cloth, paper, and wood, the majority being on cloth. The greater part of these were done by anonymous priest-painters or by commissioned laymen and were acts of religious devotion rather than of conscious artistic creation; they were originally intended to serve as aids in religious instruction or to inspire those who came to the temple. The subjects of most of the cloth paintings are the life of the Buddha (the large paintings in the stairhall, for example) or the Jataka story of Prince Vessantara (the paintings in the dining room), which of all the 547 Jataka stories is probably the most popular in Thailand. This tale tells the varied adventures of the selfless Prince Vessantara, who to achieve perfection gave away all his possessions, including his wife and children, and is usually depicted in a set of thirteen paintings, illustrating the thirteen cantos of the story. Several legends have grown up about the painting of a set of illustrations of the *Vessantara Jataka*. According to one, the painter would go insane if he attempted to do more than one complete set; another warns that his life work would be over and he would die if he finished one. Whatever the explanation, one of the paintings in many Vessantara sets is in fact incomplete, with a missing column on a temple or a small, unpainted section.

The smaller paintings on paper, which resemble Indian or Persian miniatures, are from prayer books on similar subjects, as well as on astrology and medical treatments; when used, they fold out accordion style.

The paintings in the gallery on the klong are not of a religious nature and have a somewhat unusual history. They were found in New York, where they had been brought by a descendant of an American missionary, Dr. J. H. Chandler, who had commissioned them to be done while he was serving in Thailand in the mid-nineteenth century. Dr. Chandler, a man of varied talents, was also one of the early American consuls to Thailand, published the first English-language newspaper (for which he introduced the first printing press), and devised the country's first steam launch, in which King Mongkut met distinguished visitors. He had the twenty-seven paintings done to provide a record of typical Thai life, a subject rarely treated in the religious art. Painted around 1860 by an unknown artist, they show such everyday scenes as coconut-gathering, rice-threshing, and activities in the village market place; the titles are in Dr. Chandler's handwriting. In addition to this unique collection of pictures, there are also four *Vessantara Jataka* paintings in the gallery.

The two paintings in the Bencharong Room, depicting the various stages in silk manufacture, are the only new paintings in the house. They were done by a young painter named Somnuk Permthongkum, one of the few present-day Thai artists who prefer to paint in the traditional style.

The porcelains in the collection are of four general kinds: Chinese, Sawankalok and Sukothai, Lopburi-Khmer, and Bencharong. The Chinese pieces range from Sung to nineteenth century, but the majority are Ming-period blue-and-white export ware. A number came from Ayudhya, where they were imported from China in the fifteenth, sixteenth, and seventeenth centuries; some of the larger pieces came from Indonesia, also an important center of Chinese trade. Sukothai and Sawankalok are names given to Thai ceramics made in the kingdom of Sukothai in the fourteenth and fifteenth centuries, using techniques taught by Chinese potters who were brought to Thailand by King Ramkangheng expressly for that purpose. They were made largely for export and have been found in both Indonesia and the Philippines. The pottery called Lopburi-Khmer, generally in a rich brown glaze, closely resembles Cambodian porcelains; it was probably made in the Lopburi area from the twelfth to the fourteenth century. Bencharong, in Thai, means "five colors" and is the name given to the brilliant pentachromatic porcelains made in China following the designs of Thai artists. These began in the seventeenth century, during the Ayudhya period, and continued into the Bangkok period in the nineteenth century. The Thompson collection of Bencharong, which is one of the most comprehensive, is displayed in a special room.

The house is furnished with many pieces of antique Thai and Chinese furniture. Among the more outstanding are the elaborately carved Chinese altar tables in the dining room and the Bencharong room, the large Thai bed in the center of the drawing room, and the seventeenth-century Chinese rosewood screen with painted glass panels in the master bedroom. There are also a number of old Thai cabinets, used originally as bookcases, painted with various scenes and floral designs. The tables in the dining room were originally gaming tables and bear the insignia of King Chulalongkorn.

The miscellaneous part of the collection is as varied as that category suggests and includes such items as a pair of wooden lions from Burma, a seventeenth-century French map of Thailand, two old Japanese bridal lamps, and a wooden Indonesian lion from Bali. One of the most charming pieces of miscellany is the splendid little mouse house in the bedroom, a fanciful structure made in the nineteenth century to house pet white mice; it so impressed one visitor to the house that she made it the subject of a children's book entitled *The Mouse Palace*.

Ideally, the Thompson house should be approached via the klong, although the expansion and modernization of Bangkok has made this difficult, if not impossible. The reason is not only that the house faces the water architecturally, as does any waterside Thai house; in addition to this, it seems to belong more to the world represented by the klongs than to the rest of the city. Somehow the Bangkok klongs that remain have managed to keep a curious quality of serenity, of timelessness, not dissimilar to that found in the walled-temple compounds. They still have trees, massive rain trees that arch over the water and long-leafed mangoes heavy in the hot season with golden fruit; and the houses along them, if usually not built in the traditional style, at least are not so determinedly up to date. The food and flower boats still go back and forth, the silk weavers still dry their ropes of brilliant thread on poles along the banks, the tempo of life has still not quite caught up with that of the avenues beyond. In such an atmosphere the house and its exotic objects are less unexpected, less of a contrast; rather, they seem a part of an established continuity.

It is certainly romantic, and perhaps unreasonable, of travelers to come to Asia in search of relief from their glass and steel cities and manufactured treasures; for Asia is, after all, a part of the modern world. Yet looking down Klong Maha Nag from the graceful little landing of the Thompson house, it is possible, if only briefly and by an effort of the imagination, to feel that the search has not been entirely in vain.

BIOGRAPHICAL NOTE

James H. W. Thompson was born in Greenville, Delaware, in 1906. He attended St. Paul's and Princeton and, after receiving his B.A. degree from Princeton in 1928, went on to study architecture at the University of Pennsylvania. He worked as an architect in New York until 1940, when he enlisted as a volunteer in the army.

During the Second World War, Mr. Thompson was assigned to the Office of Strategic Services, and it was in this capacity that he first came to Asia and, eventually, to Thailand. He was in Ceylon when the war ended, training with a group that was scheduled to be parachuted into Thailand to assist in the liberation of the country; he arrived in Bangkok by more conventional means two days after V-J Day and liked the country so much that later, on being discharged from the service, he decided to return and make it his home.

In the early part of his residence he was active in the reorganization of the old Oriental Hotel. Also in 1946, he became interested in the commercial possibilities of Thai silk, a lustrous, handwoven fabric that had once been produced in quantity but that had been almost displaced by competition from cheap machine-made goods. Only

1–4. James Thompson at his Bangkok home, 1967

a few families were at that time still in the silk-weaving business, mostly in an old section of Bangkok called Bang Krua, across the klong from the site of the present Thompson house.

Mr. Thompson was convinced that the beauty and quality of the silk would have an appeal outside of Thailand, and accordingly he gathered as many samples as he could find and went to New York to see what interest they would stir among sophisticated buyers. The response was sufficiently encouraging for him to return to Bangkok and, on a small investment, to found the Thai Silk Company Ltd., of which he became managing director. To the ancient manufacturing process he introduced modern dyes and new designs and also set standards of production; the actual weaving, however, continued to be done largely in homes on a cottage-industry basis, just as it had in the past.

The venture was a notable success. Within a few years, Thai silk had become a well-known luxury item throughout the world, extensively used in fashion and interior decoration as well as in the theater (*The King and I*) and films (*Ben Hur*). With the founding of several hundred other independent silk companies in Bangkok, it also became one of Thailand's outstanding export commodities and perhaps the country's most famous single product. During the 1950's, Mr. Thompson went several times to Burma by invitation to advise that country in its textile industry, and in 1962, in recognition of his contribution to Thailand, the Thai government awarded him the Order of the White Elephant.

At the same time he was developing his silk business, he also became increasingly interested in Thai architecture and Southeast Asian art, and the result was the house and collection pictured in this book. The house, known in Bangkok simply as "Jim Thompson's House," has become a leading tourist attraction and is open to the public twice a week, the proceeds going to a local charity.

Over the Easter weekend in 1967, Mr. Thompson disappeared while on a holiday with friends in the northern Malaysian resort of the Cameron Highlands. An extensive and continuing search has so far failed to discover clues or information concerning the disappearance of this remarkable man who achieved so much in such a variety of fields.

5. *Limestone torso of the* ▷
Buddha, Dvaravati style

6. *The house: high-angle view*

8. *The house from the klong*

18

7. The house: front view

9. *The drawing room*

10. The dining room

11. Blue-and-white porcelains of the Ming dynasty

12. *The master bedroom*

13. *Figure of Hari-Hara,* ▷
Sukothai style

24

14. Head of Suriya, the sun god, pre-Angkor style

15. *Head of Siva, Khmer style*

16. *Head of Hari-Hara,*
    Khmer style

17. Head of Ardhanari,
Khmer style: three views

18. *Enlargement of 19, left figure*

19. *Three dancing figures, Khmer style*

21. Figure of Hanuman,
Khmer style

20. Siva and Uma on their
bull Nandi, Khmer style

23. *Objects in the study*

◁ 22. *Figure of a Bodhisattva,*
pre-Angkor style

24. *Chinese rain drum*

25. *Figure of Chanda-li: five views*

26–27. *Figure of Vishnu on a garuda, Khmer style: two views*

28. *Gold votive plaque, pre-Angkor style*

29. *Gold votive plaque,*
    Sukothai style

30–31. *Gold votive plaques,*
       Founan style

32. *Gold votive plaque,*
    pre-Angkor style

33. *Gold votive plaque, Ayudhya style*

34. Figure of Vishnu,
   Khmer style

35. Figure of a Bodhi-
sattva, Srivijaya style

36. Figure of Uma,
   Khmer style ▷

37. *The study*

38. *Seated Buddha, Lopburi-Khmer style* ▷

◁ 39. Detail o,
Uma figure,
Khmer style

40. Figures of
Siva and Uma,
Khmer style

42. Head of the Buddha, U-Thong style

◁ *41. Standing Buddha,*
Dvaravati style

43. Detail of Hari-Hara, Sukothai style

44. Detail of Hari-Hara, Sukothai style ▷

46. Painting of a scene from the Vessantara Jataka, *Bangkok period*

◁ *45. The entrance hall*

47. *Painting of a scene from the* Vessantara Jataka, *Bangkok period*

48. *Painting of a scene from the* ▷
Vessantara Jataka, *Chiengmai style*

49. Painting showing scenes of daily life, Ayudhya style

50. Bencharong porcelain

51

52

55

56

51–58. Scenes from the Vessantara Jataka, *Bangkok period*

54

53

54

57

58

60. Head of a female deity, Khmer style

◁ *59. A selection of Thai ceramics*

61. *Votive plaque, Dvaravati style*

63. *Figure of a Brahmin ▷ priest, Sukothai style*

62. *Figure of a king or chieftain, Khmer style*

64. Figure of Prajnaparamita, Khmer style

65. *Head of a Dhammapala, Khmer style*

66. Carved pediment panel, Ayudhya style

67. Three Thai jars in the garden ▷

68. *Seated bronze Buddha,*
   Khmer style

69. *Figure of the Buddha,* ▷
   Lopburi-Khmer style

◁ 70. The Buddha flanked by two disciples, Ayudhya style

71. Standing ▷ wooden Buddha, Ayudhya style

72. Part of the Bencharong collection, backed by a Burmese tapestry

73. *Bencharong bowl with Chinese design*

74. *Cover of Bencharong bowl*

75. *Bencharong bowl with typical Thai design*

76. Painting gallery in the garden

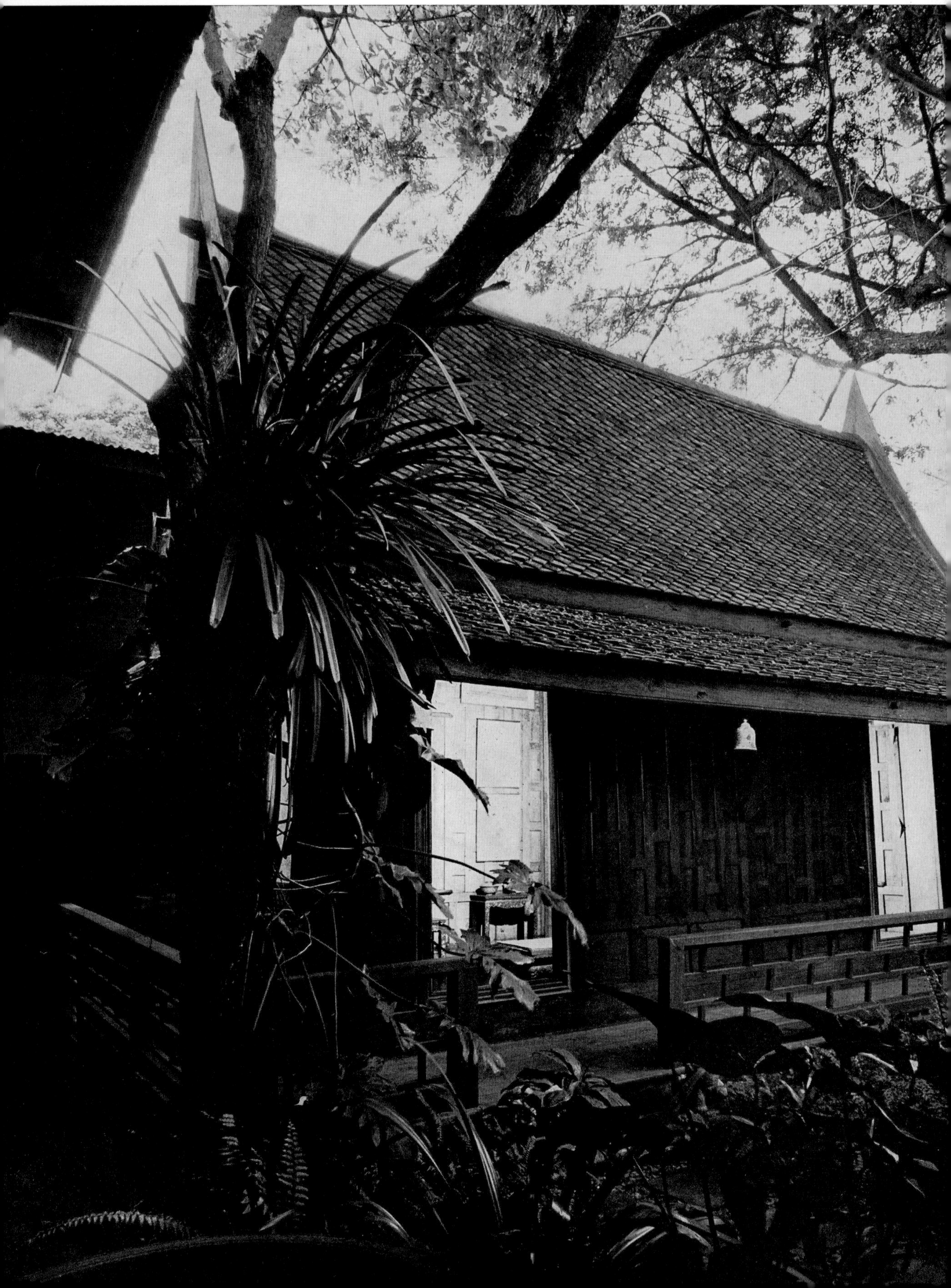

77. Demon, Khmer style

78. Wooden mouse house, Bangkok period

71

79. *Seated Burmese Buddha in the drawing room*

80. *Carved figure of a Burmese spirit* ▷

82. *Kneeling priest, Burmese*

◁ 83. A pair of 6th-
century stone deer
in the garden

84. *Khmer-style stone squirrel on a rain jar*

*85. The house
in the evening*

*86. Bronze votive plaque set in
a wooden frame, Sukothai style*

FLOOR PLAN OF THE MAIN HOUSE

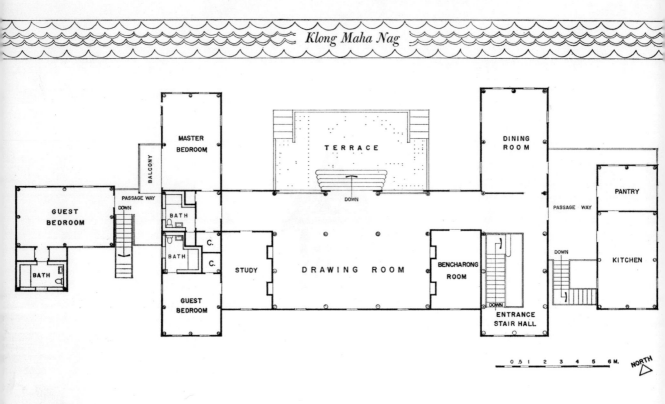

Klong Maha Nag

ART PERIODS OF THAILAND

Dvaravati style	6th to 10th century
Haripunjay style	8th to 12th century
Khmer-Lopburi style	10th to 14th century
Early Chiengsen style	12th to 14th century
U-Thong style	13th to 15th century
Sukothai style	13th to 15th century
Late Chiengsen style	14th century to present
Ayudhya style	14th to 18th century
Bangkok (Ratanakosin) style	18th century to present

COMMENTARIES ON THE PLATES

TITLE PAGE. View of the Thompson house from across the klong.

1–4. James Thompson plays with Cocky, his pet cockatoo, on the veranda of his Bangkok home early in 1967.

5. Standing torso. Limestone. Height 115 cm. Dvaravati style, early 6th century. This torso, said by several authorities to be one of the earliest Buddhist images found in Southeast Asia, came from Lopburi province.

6–8. Three views of the Thompson house. From left to right: high-angle view, front view, and view from the klong.

9. The drawing room.

10. The dining room.

11. Blue-and-white porcelains. All but one of the porcelains shown are Annamese; the small bowl in the center front is Chinese. All were made during the Ming dynasty.

12. The master bedroom.

13. Figure of Hari-Hara. Bronze.

Height 76 cm. Sukothai style, 14th century. Hari-Hara is a deity who combines Vishnu and Siva in one god.

14. Head of Suriya. Limestone. Height 39 cm. Pre-Angkor style, late 7th or early 8th century. Suriya was known as the Sun God; this head came from Cholburi province.

15. Head of Siva. Limestone. Height 22.5 cm. Khmer style, 11th century.

16. Head of Hari-Hara. Sandstone. Height 13 cm. Khmer style, 8th century. From Cambodia.

17. Head of Ardhanari: three views. Limestone. Height 36.5 cm. Khmer style, 10th century. This deity is half male (Siva) and half female (Uma) and is in the style of Koh Ker, Cambodia.

18. Enlargement of 19, left figure.

19. Three dancing figures. Bronze. Left figure is 22.5 cm. tall, center figure is 18.5 cm. tall, and right figure is 25 cm. tall. All three are Khmer style; the right figure is 13th century and the other two are 10th century. The three, which came from Cambodia, were

originally the tops of battle standards.

20. Figure of Siva and Uma on their bull Nandi. Bronze. Height 10 cm. From Cambodia.

21. Figure of Hanuman. Bronze. Height 16 cm. Khmer style, 13th century. This figure of the monkey god was the top of a Cambodian battle standard.

22. Figure of the Bodhisattva Padmapani. Bronze. Height 25.5 cm. Pre-Angkor style, late 7th or early 8th century. This figure came from Buriram province.

23. A group of objects in the study, with a view of the garden.

24. Chinese rain drum. Bronze. Height 18 cm., diameter 16.5 cm. Sung dynasty.

25. Figure of Chanda-li: five views. Bronze. Height 17 cm. Khmer style, 11th century. Chanda-li, a female Tantric Buddhist deity, is one of the goddesses known as *yogini;* she is sometimes called the Destroyer of Ignorance. She holds a discus in her right hand and a ploughshare across her breast. From Korat province.

26–27. Figure of Vishnu on a *garuda:* two views. Bronze. Height 14.5 cm. Khmer style, 13th century. The *garuda* was the king of birds and the usual mount of Vishnu; in the Bangkok period it became the emblem of Thailand.

28. Votive plaque. Gold. Height 7 cm. Pre-Angkor style, 7th century. This

plaque, which contains a Sanskrit inscription, came from Petchaboon province.

29. Votive plaque. Gold. Height 7 cm. Sukothai style, 14th-15th century. The figure on this plaque is a walking Buddha with distinctive Sukothai features.

30–31. Votive plaques. Gold. Diameter 4 cm. Founan style, 4th–5th century. Shown on these two plaques, which came from U-Thong province, are deities seated in the Javanese fashion. There are also Sanskrit inscriptions on them.

32. Votive plaque. Gold. Height 8 cm. Pre-Angkor style, 7th century. This plaque shows the Bodhisattva Maitreya and was brought from Petchaboon province.

33. Votive plaque. Gold. Height 5 cm. Ayudhya style, 15th century. This plaque shows the Buddha together with two attendants seated under the sacred tree.

34. Figure of Vishnu. Sandstone. Height 70 cm. Khmer style, 12th century. From Surin province.

35. Figure of a Bodhisattva. Tin and silver alloy. Height 41 cm. Srivijaya style, 8th–9th century. This figure is the Bodhisattva Maitreya, the Buddha-to-be; it came from a private collection in Bangkok.

36. Figure of Uma. Sandstone. Height 83.5 cm. Khmer style, 11th century. From Paktongchai, Korat province.

37. The study, with a view of the garden.

38. Seated Buddha. Sandstone. Height 81.5 cm. Lopburi-Khmer style, 13th century. From Supanburi province.

39. Detail of the figure of Uma pictured on page 43.

40. Figures of Siva and Uma. Limestone. The Siva figure is 59.5 cm. tall and the Uma figure 60.5 cm. Both are Khmer style, 12th century. From Surin province.

41. Standing Buddha. Limestone. Height 104 cm. Dvaravati style, 6th century. From Lopburi province.

42. Head of the Buddha. Sandstone. Height 44.5 cm. U-Thong style, late 13th century. This image came from Singhburi province.

43. Detail of the figure of Hari-Hara shown on page 25.

44. Enlarged detail of Hari-Hara.

45. View of the entrance hall, looking toward the Dvaravati-stye torso in the garden.

46. Scene from the *Vessantara Jataka*. Cloth. Width 34 cm., height 41 cm. Bangkok period, late 18th or early 19th century. This scene from the popular Vessantara legend shows Prince Vessantara, his wife, and his two children riding into exile.

47. Scene from the *Vessantara Jataka*. Cloth. Width 51 cm., height 60 cm. Bangkok period, early 19th century. In this scene, Prince Vessantara, on his journey into exile, pauses for a rest.

48. Scene from the *Vessantara Jataka*. Koi paper. Width 56.5 cm, height 81.5 cm. From Chiengmai, early 19th century. This scene shows Prince Vessantara's return from exile.

49. Scenes of daily life. Width 33 cm., height 38 cm. Ayudhya style, 18th century. Thai paintings are normally of a religious nature. This is a rare exception, showing scenes from the daily life of Thai and Karen people.

50. A selection from the Bencharong collection, showing typical shapes and designs. Bencharong, which means "five colors" in Thai, is the name given to porcelains made in China following the designs of Thai artists; they were first made in the 17th century, during the Ayudhya period, and continued into the Bangkok period.

51–58. Scenes from the *Vessantara Jataka*. Width 41.5 cm., height 48 cm. Bangkok period, early 19th century. The eight paintings on these pages are from the same set showing scenes in the popular legend, which tells the story of Prince Vessantara, who achieved perfection by giving away all his possessions. Number 51 shows the goddess Indra asking Vessantara's mother to return to earth to bear the holy child. Number 52 shows Vessantara giving away his white elephant. Number 53 shows him giving away his chariot. In number 54 he is seen walking with his wife and children in the forest, after giving away his worldly possessions. Number 55 shows the mocking of the new wife of the hermit who later takes Vessantara's children. In number 56, the hermit is seen asking the way to Vessantara's retreat. Number 57 shows Vessantara's triumphant return, and number 58 shows him reunited at last at home.

59. A selection of Thai ceramics. All but the bowl at upper left are Sawankalok, made in the kingdom of Sukothai in the late 14th and 15th centuries. The exception was made somewhat later in Samkampeng, near Chiengmai, by potters employing similar techniques.

60. Head of a female deity. Sandstone. Height 19 cm. Khmer style, 11th century. From Ubol province.

61. Votive plaque. Terra cotta. Width 8.5 cm., height 12 cm. Dvaravati style, 8th–10th century. From Nakorn Sawan province.

62. Figure of a king or chieftain. Bronze. Height 16.5 cm. Khmer style, 11th century. From a private collection in Lopburi.

63. Figure of a Brahmin priest. Bronze. Height 18 cm. Sukothai style, 14th century. From a private collection in Bangkok.

64. Figure of Prajnaparamita. Bronze. Height 36 cm. Khmer style, 13th century. In Mahayana Buddhism, Prajnaparamita is considered to be the Mother of All Buddhas and also the Goddess of Wisdom. This image came from Buriram province.

65. Head of a Dhammapala. Red sandstone. Height 41.5 cm. Khmer style, late 13th century. The Dhammapala are defenders of the Buddhist faith. From Korat province.

66. Carved panel. Wood. Height 33 cm., length 34.5 cm. Ayudhya style, 18th century. This panel was originally part of a pediment and depicts a scene from the legend of "Pra Malai," a poem composed in the 18th century. Pra Malai is a monk who visits both heaven and hell to view their rewards and punishments. Here he is seen ascending to heaven.

67. Thai jars in the garden. The piece on the left is Chalieng style, 14th–15th century; the center piece is Lopburi-Khmer style, 13th–14th century; the one on the right is Sawankalok style, 15th century.

68. Seated Buddha. Bronze. Height 20 cm. Khmer style, 13th century. This image, found in Lopburi province, is in the attitude of calling the earth to witness and is in the attributes of royalty.

69. Figure of the Buddha in the attributes of royalty. Bronze. Height 50 cm. Lopburi-Khmer style, 13th century. This serene figure of the Buddha is shown making a double gesture in the position of teaching and came from Lopburi.

70. The Buddha holding a fan and flanked by two disciples. Sandstone.